Girls Got Game

girls' **GOLF**

Teeing It Up

by Heather E. Schwartz

Consultant
Nancy Bender, LPGA Teacher of the Year, 2003
A Top 50 Teacher in the Nation in *Golf for Women Magazine* 2001-2007

Capstone
press®

Mankato, Minnesota

Snap Books are published by Capstone Press,
151 Good Counsel Drive, P.O. Box 669, Mankato, Minnesota 56002.
www.capstonepress.com

Library of Congress Cataloging-in-Publication Data

Schwartz, Heather E.
   Girls' golf: teeing it up / Heather E. Schwartz.
   p. cm.—(Snap books. Girls got game)
   Summary: "Describes golf, the skills needed for it, and ways to
compete"—Provided by publisher.
   Includes bibliographical references and index.
   ISBN-13: 978-1-4296-0132-0 (hardcover)
   ISBN-10: 1-4296-0132-9 (hardcover)
   1. Golf for women—Juvenile literature. 2. Golf for children—Juvenile
literature. I. Title. II. Series.
GV966.S394 2008
796.352082—dc22   2007000900

Editors: Kendra Christensen and Becky Viaene

Designer: Bobbi J. Wyss

Photo Researchers: Charlene Deyle and Scott Thoms

Photo Credits: AP Photo, 27; AP Photo/Chris Carlson, 10; AP Photo/
Jay LaPrete, 16; AP Photo/John Bazemore, 5; AP Photo/Laurence Harris, 26;
AP Photo/Themba Hadebe, 19, 21; AP Photo/Vincent Thian, 23; Capstone
Press/Karon Dubke, 11 (all); Comstock Inc., back cover (bag of clubs); Corbis/
Dallas Morning News/Michael Ainsworth, 28; Corbis/David Bergman, 25;
Corbis/Reuters/Ian Hodgson, cover, 29; Hot Shots Photo, 32; Index Stock
Imagery/Bill Bachmann, 14–15; iStockphoto/Jan Tyler, 17; Shutterstock/
BarbaraJH, 7; Shutterstock/Jay Kim, 13; Shutterstock/John, 8–9

1 2 3 4 5 6 12 11 10 09 08 07

TABLE OF CONTENTS

CHAPTER ONE

GET OUT ON THE GREEN

So many sports are about running, jumping, and speeding your way to the top. But if those activities aren't your thing, you're not doomed to sit on the sidelines. Golf taps into other talents, like superior concentration skills and amazing aim. After all, just one stroke can win or lose a game of golf. A girl who knows how to focus will find she's got a competitive edge on the course.

Perfecting your game takes time and practice. Just keep practicing to improve your skills, challenging yourself against other golfers, and enjoying the game. It won't be long before you're swinging your way to the top.

Annika
Sorenstam

It's a Brain Game

In golf, having a positive mental attitude is as important as being physically fit. The game definitely gets physical—it takes flexibility to swing the club properly and power to send the ball sailing. But it's a mental game too.

So what's going on in a great golfer's head? Before a golfer even swings her club, she's imagining the shot she's about to make. The picture in her mind shows it all happening perfectly. When she begins to swing, she's completely focused. Most importantly, she knows how much a good attitude counts in this game. No matter how she plays, a good golfer is calm and positive from the first tee to her last stroke.

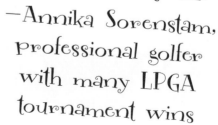

"I believe in positive thinking, believing in yourself. I push myself to be the best that I can be. I don't worry about what other people are doing, and I don't think about things I can't control."
—Annika Sorenstam, professional golfer with many LPGA tournament wins

7

CHAPTER TWO

PLAYING BY THE RULES

Feel free to whack the ball 20 times if that's what it takes to get it in the hole. Just remember, your goal is to sink the ball with the fewest strokes, or swings, of your club. In stroke play, the golfer with the fewest strokes at the end of the game wins. In match play, scoring is done at each hole. The player with the fewest strokes at a hole wins that hole. The player who wins the most holes wins the match.

Each hole has a set number of strokes to sink the ball, called par. Even better than getting par is getting an eagle, which is two strokes under par. A birdie is one under par. But a bogey, one over par, isn't bad either.

Par for the Course

Par is determined by the distance from the tee to the hole.

Distance from tee to hole	Par
under 240 yards (219 meters)	3
up to 450 yards (411 meters)	4
450-650 yards (411-594 meters)	5

Tee Time

Ready for a round of golf? A typical round is 18 holes, but you may want to start by playing only 9 holes. For each hole, players take turns sending the ball from the tee to the green, where the hole is located. Between the tee and the green is the fairway. The distance from tee to hole could be as far as 600 yards (549 meters). That's about the length of five football fields! Luckily, each player has 14 clubs and can choose the right one to make her best shot.

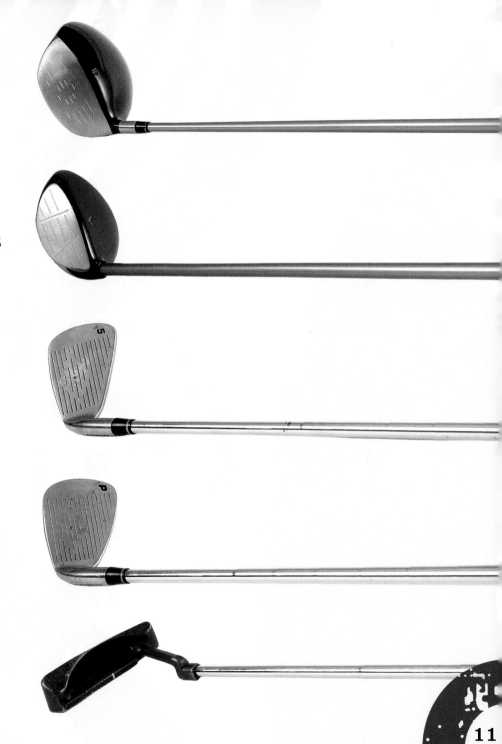

Driver

The driver, or number one wood, is used at the tee. It helps golfers shoot the farthest.

Woods

Woods, other than drivers, are used far from the hole on the fairway. They can help golfers shoot 180 yards (165 meters) or more.

Irons

Irons are used closer to the hole on the fairway. They can help golfers shoot 100 to 170 yards (91 to 155 meters).

Pitching Wedge

A pitching wedge is used close to the hole on the fairway. It can pop the ball in the air and make it travel about 90 yards (82 meters).

Putter

A putter is used on the green. It makes the ball roll to the hole.

Good Manners Aren't Just for Dinner

On the golf course, rules of polite behavior are a big deal. Golf etiquette guidelines include:

- Quiet please. When it's one golfer's turn to shoot, everyone else should be quiet. Even a shadow could be distracting, so step back and watch from a distance.

- Remember to clean up your mess before you leave. Sometimes golfers rip up pieces of ground, called divots, when they swing their clubs. Players should replace divots before moving on.

- Look before you swing. Don't swing until you're sure there's no one nearby who could be hit by the club or the ball.

- Yes, there's a dress code. Most golf courses frown upon clothing that's too casual, like tank tops and short shorts. Try a collared shirt and longer shorts instead. Sneakers or golf shoes are a must.

Did someone yell "four?"

Actually, the word is "fore" and it's a warning. It means watch out because a ball's coming your way!

CHAPTER THREE

HITTING THE COURSE

Let's say you're a pretty good beginner, but for now, your friends are way better golfers than you are. Playing with them wouldn't be much fun, since you'd be sure to lose, right? Wrong!

In golf, there's a system called handicapping. It lets you have a few extra strokes on each hole, allowing you to compete against players with better abilities.

Your handicap gives you an opportunity to win any game fair and square. But there's another reason to play golf with stronger players. You're bound to pick up pointers that will improve your game and lower your handicap too.

Improving Your Golf Game

You'll need strong muscles and flexibility to swing with power and precision. Try tennis to strengthen those arm muscles. Swimming will improve endurance. With exercise, you'll be in top form on the golf course.

It's hot, I'm tired, and I keep missing the ball!

If you're frustrated at first, don't feel bad. It's not easy for beginners to aim the ball toward the hole—or even hit the ball at all. Golf takes practice. A good instructor can help you improve your game. Look for junior golf programs in your community or take lessons at a golf course. Proper stance, accurate aim, and an excellent swing rarely come naturally. But with practice, any girl can learn these skills—and that includes you.

50

How can I improve my game?

Practice! If you want to improve your longer shots, head to the driving range. Rent a bucket of balls and spend time shooting into the long field. It's marked off in yards, so you can see how far your ball travels. Try to make it go farther each time. Playing miniature golf is a great way to work on your putting skills. On the larger course, you'll use those same skills on the green.

Tournament Time

Ready to compete against other players? In competitive tournaments, golfers don't just play 9 holes. They don't even stick to a single round of 18 holes. They play even more, competing in several 18-hole rounds. Challenging? No doubt. But the good news is tournaments aren't played all at once. They take place over a few days. They also include practice rounds so you can brush up on your skills right before you compete.

Hole in One

A hole in one is an incredible accomplishment for anyone. But shooting the ball from the tee directly into the hole is very difficult, so keep practicing.

CHAPTER FOUR

BECOMING THE BEST

Try out for your high school golf team, and you'll have a chance to show school spirit and improve your game. You'll also get a chance to become friends with other girls who love golf. During the school year, you'll get to compete against other school teams. You could even make it to a state tournament or national championship.

But even if you play on your high school team, you still have the whole summer free. High school golfers hoping to score a college scholarship know it makes sense to play year-round. College coaches scout summer events, especially state and national tournaments, for strong players who'll fit in on their teams.

Competitions

Test yourself by competing against other junior players in community programs, like LPGA-USGA Girls Golf. Girls ages 7 to 17 can get involved. While play is competitive, the focus is on learning and having fun.

Serious junior golfers compete in community, regional, and state events. That's the path to national tournaments, like those sponsored by the American Junior Golf Association (AJGA). To play in an AJGA event you'll need to be between 12 and 18 years old. AJGA offers young athletes the opportunity to play in competitive events and get the exposure needed to earn college scholarships.

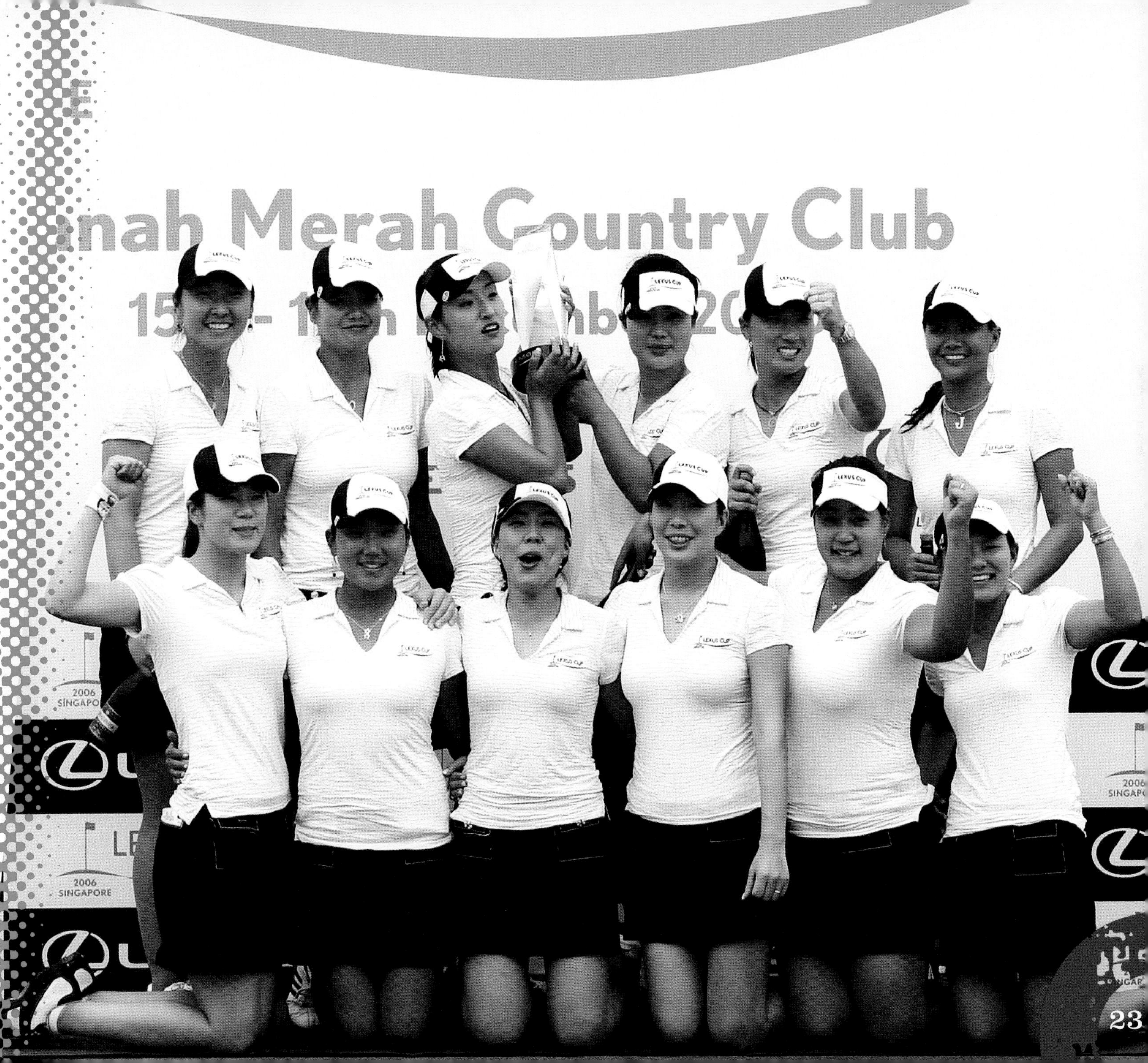
Merah Country Club
2006
SINGAPORE
2006
SINGAPORE

Going Pro

Once you've been playing golf for a while, you may start dreaming of being a professional golfer one day. With lots of practice, some women golfers become pros. They earn a spot on the Duramed FUTURES Tour, a professional tour for ages 17 and older. Players on the tour are truly dedicated to the game. They put in about eight to 10 hours on the course each day, six days a week. After a few years, some earn a spot on the LPGA Tour, the highest level of play for women golfers. Those who make it on the LPGA Tour play golf at events all around the world.

Paula Creamer

 My expectations are incredibly high. I put the most pressure on myself. I'm not normally content with what I do unless I win. I've always looked forward to turning pro.
—Paula Creamer, professional golfer and LPGA tournament winner

CHAPTER FIVE

PRO PLAYERS

Becoming a great golfer can be a big challenge—especially if you're new to the game. Some of the best women golfers in history faced challenges of their own to become great golfers.

Mildred "Babe" Didrikson Zaharias was an awesome athlete. She was nicknamed "Babe" after Babe Ruth for her home run hitting skills in baseball. In 1932, she won gold and silver medals for track and field at the Olympics. In 1935, at the age of 21, Zaharias decided to try golf. She wound up winning 55 amateur and professional golf tournaments and helped found the LPGA in 1950.

Mildred Didrikson Zaharias

Marlene Bauer Hagge

Marlene Bauer Hagge learned to walk and soon after learned to golf. In 1937, the 3-year-old joined her dad on the golf course. As Hagge got older, she enjoyed the game, but faced a major obstacle. Junior golf programs for girls didn't exist then. No quitter, she mastered the game by golfing with boys and men. Hagge went on to become the youngest player ever to win an LPGA event in 1952 at age 18. But Hagge didn't quit playing after that. She continued competing until 1996. In 2002, Hagge became a member of the World Golf Hall of Fame.

Annika Sorenstam

Annika Sorenstam started golfing at age 12. Sorenstam impressed everyone in 2001, when she became the first female golfer to achieve golf's lowest score, a 59. In 2003, Sorenstam made history when she challenged top male golfers on the PGA Tour. Women aren't usually expected to shoot from the same tee as men. They start a little closer to the hole. But Sorenstam shot from the same spot as the men and played without a handicap too.

Michelle Wie started playing golf at age 4. By 11, she was spending about three hours a day on the course on weekdays and eight hours a day on weekends. Practice paid off. In 2002, Wie was the youngest player to qualify for the LPGA Tour at age 12. Now she's a big-time professional golfer. Wie's next goal is to play in the PGA Tour. Wie says, "I like challenges and I just have to be the first to do everything, and I just want to be the best."

Michelle Wie

So you see? Even the best golfers need to work hard to rise to the top. Practice your swings, perfect your aim, and your game is sure to improve!

GLOSSARY

fairway (FAIR-way)—the area between the tee and the green

green (GREEN)—a closely mowed area where a golf hole is located

handicap (HAN-dee-kap)—an advantage given to less skilled golfers to make competition more equal

par (PAR)—the number of strokes it should take to get the ball into the hole

putt (PUHT)—to hit a golf ball lightly into the hole

tee (TEE)—a small wooden peg that the golf ball is set on

FAST FACTS

Years ago, women golfers played in blouses and ankle-length skirts.

The word "golf" comes from the Dutch word for club.

The little dimples covering golf balls aren't just decorative. They actually trap pockets of air to help the balls fly.

The World Golf Hall of Fame is located in St. Augustine, Florida. It honors the greatest golfers. By 2006, 114 men and women, including Marlene Bauer Hagge, Annika Sorenstam, and Mildred "Babe" Didrikson Zaharias, were members.

READ MORE

Ditchfield, Christin. *Golf.* A True Book. Danbury, Conn.: Children's Press, 2003.

Frisch, Aaron. *Golf.* World of Sports. North Mankato, Minn.: Smart Apple Media, 2003.

Krause, Peter. *Play-by-Play Golf.* Play-by-Play. Minneapolis: Lerner, 2002.

Thomas, Ron, and Joe Herran. *Getting into Golf.* Philadelphia: Chelsea House, 2005.

INTERNET SITES

FactHound offers a safe, fun way to find Internet sites related to this book. All of the sites on FactHound have been researched by our staff.

Here's how:

1. Visit *www.facthound.com*

2. Choose your grade level.

3. Type in this book ID **1429601329** for age-appropriate sites. You may also browse subjects by clicking on letters, or by clicking on pictures and words.

4. Click on the **Fetch It** button.

Facthound will fetch the best sites for you!

ABOUT THE AUTHOR

Heather E. Schwartz is a freelance writer based in upstate New York. Her favorite things to write about include sports, fitness, and health. She especially likes writing for kids' publications like *National Geographic Kids*, *Girls' Life,* and *Teen*. Heather also teaches workshops for girls through Girls Inc., a national nonprofit youth organization.When Heather isn't at her computer, she likes to ski, hike, bike, read, and play the violin. She's no pro, but she also enjoys playing golf—especially miniature golf!

INDEX